MAY   2005

EASY   Williams, Linda
Wheels   D.
Wil   Concrete
            mixers

Pebble™
Plus

Mighty Machines
Concrete Mixers

by Linda D. Williams

Consulting Editor: Gail Saunders-Smith, PhD
Consultant: Debra Hilmerson, Member
American Society of Safety Engineers
Des Plaines, Illinois

Capstone
press

Mankato, Minnesota

Pebble Plus is published by Capstone Press
151 Good Counsel Drive, P.O. Box 669, Mankato, Minnesota 56002
www.capstonepress.com

1 2 3 4 5 6 09 08 07 06 05 04

Library of Congress Cataloging-in-Publication Data
Williams, Linda D.
    Concrete mixers / by Linda D. Williams.
    p. cm.—(Pebble plus: mighty machines)
    Includes bibliographical references and index.
    ISBN 0-7368-2594-0 (hardcover)
    1. Concrete mixers—Juvenile literature. [1. Concrete mixers.] I. Title. II. Series.
TA439.W4595 2005
624.1'834—dc22   2003025764

Summary: Simple text and photographs present concrete mixers and the work they do.

Editorial Credits
Martha E. H. Rustad, editor; Molly Nei, designer; Scott Thoms, photo researcher;
    Karen Hieb, product planning editor

Photo Credits
Bruce Coleman Inc./Wendell Metzen, 13
Capstone Press/Gary Sundermeyer, cover
constructionphotography.com, 15
Corbis/Vince Streano, 4–5
David R. Frazier Photolibrary, 7, 16–17, 18–19, 21
Index Stock Imagery/Aneal Vohra, 10–11; Wendell Metzen, 8–9
Laura N. Scott Imagery, 1

Note to Parents and Teachers

The Mighty Machines series supports national standards related to science, technology, and society. This book describes and illustrates concrete mixers. The images support early readers in understanding the text. The repetition of words and phrases helps early readers learn new words. This book also introduces early readers to subject-specific vocabulary words, which are defined in the Glossary section. Early readers may need assistance to read some words and to use the Table of Contents, Glossary, Read More, Internet Sites, and Index/Word List sections of the book.

Word Count: 110
Early-Intervention Level: 12

Table of Contents

Concrete Mixers. 4

Concrete Mixer Parts 10

Using Concrete 18

Mighty Machines 20

Glossary. 22

Read More 23

Internet Sites 23

Index/Word List. 24

Concrete Mixers

Concrete mixers mix and
pour concrete.

Concrete mixers keep
concrete soft. Concrete gets
hard when it sits and dries.

Machines load wet concrete
into concrete mixers. Concrete
mixers carry concrete
to building sites.

9

Concrete Mixer Parts

Concrete mixers have drums.
Drums turn and mix the
wet concrete inside.

drum

Concrete mixer drivers sit in cabs. Drivers control the spinning drum.

cab

Concrete pours out
of concrete mixers on
chutes. Concrete mixers
move on tires.

chute

Pumper trucks pump concrete from concrete mixers. Pumper trucks pour concrete through long hoses.

pumper truck

Using Concrete

Builders smooth and form concrete. They make driveways and sidewalks. They make roads and airport runways.

Mighty Machines

Concrete mixers mix and pour concrete. Concrete mixers are mighty machines.

Glossary

building site—a place where something new is being made or constructed

cab—an area for a driver to sit in a large truck or machine, such as a concrete mixer

chute—a narrow slide; concrete pours out of concrete mixers on chutes.

concrete—a mixture of cement, water, sand, and small rocks; concrete hardens as it sits and dries.

drum—a turning container that mixes concrete

hose—a long plastic tube; concrete moves through a hose on a boom from a pumper truck.

pumper truck—a vehicle with a long hose that is used for pouring concrete; pumper trucks pour concrete for tall buildings and bridges.

runway—an area of flat, paved ground where airplanes take off and land

Read More

Eick, Jean. *Concrete Mixers.* Big Machines at Work. Eden Prairie, Minn.: Child's World, 1999.

Nelson, Robin. *From Cement to Bridge.* Start to Finish. Minneapolis: Lerner Publications, 2004.

Randolph, Joanne. *Concrete Mixers.* Road Machines. New York: PowerKids Press, 2002.

Internet Sites

FactHound offers a safe, fun way to find Internet sites related to this book. All of the sites on FactHound have been researched by our staff.

Here's how:

1. Visit *www.facthound.com*

2. Type in this special code **0736825940** for age-appropriate sites. Or enter a search word related to this book for a more general search.

3. Click on the **Fetch It** button.

FactHound will fetch the best sites for you!

Index/Word List

builders, 18

building, 8

cabs, 12

chutes, 14

concrete, 4, 6, 8, 10, 14,
  16, 18, 20

control, 12

drivers, 12

driveways, 18

drum, 10, 12

hard, 6

hoses, 16

machines, 8, 20

mix, 4, 10, 20

move, 14

pour, 4, 14, 16, 20

pumper trucks, 16

roads, 18

runways, 18

sidewalks, 18

sites, 8

smooth, 18

soft, 6

spinning, 12

tires, 14

wet, 8, 10